BOOK OF POETRY

BOOK OF POETRY

MARIANNE LAIRD

To order additional copies of this book, contact:
Xlibris
UK TFN: 0800 0148620 (Toll Free inside the UK)
UK Local: 02036 956328 (+44 20 3695 6328 from outside the UK)
www.Xlibrispublishing.co.uk
Orders@Xlibrispublishing.co.uk
816195

CONTENTS

FREEDOM

THE MORNING ARRIVES AS I SAY WOW
WHAT A BEAUTIFUL DAY,
AS NOW I AM LEARNING TO LIVE FOR EACH MOMENT
BEFORE IT BECOMES THE PAST,
I FEEL I CAN START LIVING AT LONG LAST
I GO FOR A WALK THE SILENCE HAS COME
BUT THEN I HEAR THE UNIVERSE TALK FROM
THE CRUNCH OF LEAVES UNDER MY FEET
TO A SOFT QUIET WHISPER OF THE WIND GO PAST
THERE REALLY IS SO MUCH CHATTER
I CAN'T EXPLAIN IT REALLY MAKES MY
HEART FLY HIGH LIKE A KITE
BLOWING FREE IN THE NIGHT
I CAN BEGIN TO HEAR WHAT PEOPLE SAY
AND JUST LISTEN TO EVERYTHING
MY BRAIN IS FREE AT LONG LAST FROM
ALL THE SELF CRITICISM
WHICH ONLY GIVES GRIEF
SO NOW WHEN THE DAY HAS BEGUN
ALL I DO IS SMILE, BREATH AND SMILE
AGAIN THEN TURN TO THE UNIVERSE AND
SAY I AM LISTENING NOW AND FREE

THE DAY HAS ENDED
AS I LAY IN MY BED

WHAT HAVE I DONE TO BRING JOY I SAY IN MY HEAD,
I DID NOTHING MY HEAD CRIES OUT WITH DESPAIR,
HOW CAN I SLEEP WITHOUT ANYTHING
GOOD I HAVE DONE FOR THE WORLD,
THEN I LOOK IN MY HEART AND REMEMBER WITH JOY,
I GAVE A SMILE TO THE OLD LADY NEXT DOOR,
BUT AS I TRY TO FALL ASLEEP,
MY MIND SAYS BIG DEAL THAT'S NOT A LOT,
I CLOSE MY EYES AND START TO CRY,
I REALLY AM NOT RIGHT IN THE HEAD,
THEN I REMEMBER THE WEE GIRL WHO FELL
FROM THE TREE AND GAVE HER A HUG,
AND HER FACE STARTED TO SMILE SO I LAY
IN MY BED AND SAID TO MYSELF
IT MIGHT NOT BE MUCH,
BUT I CAN TRY HARDER TOMORROW,
SO MY MIND SLOWS DOWN AS I FALL TO SLEEP,
AND REMEMBER ALL THE GOOD THINGS I DID IN THE DAY,
WHICH MADE ME FEEL BETTER TO START A NEW DAY OUT,
SO WHEN YOU LIE IN YOUR BED JUST LIKE ME,

JUST REMEMBER THE JOY YOU GIVE TO ALL
THESE PEOPLE YOU DO NOT KNOW,
AS MAYBE ONE DAY THEY WILL HELP YOU,
AND THEY WILL WAKE UP FEELING GREAT NOT BLUE,

HABIT

I GET UP IN THE MORNING AT HALF PAST FIVE,
I HAVE DONE THIS ALL MY LIFE,
I PUT THE KETTLE ON WHILE I WASH AND DRESS,
THEN BUTTER MY TOAST AND TRY NOT TO MAKE A MESS,
EVERY MORNING CRUMBS ALL AROUND,
I SWEEP THEM IN A HURRY THEN RUSH FOR MY BUS,
AS I LEAVE MY HOUSE I SEE THE BUS GO BY,
SO I BEGIN TO PANIC AND START TO CRY,
THEN I JUST GO BACK HOME,
ANOTHER DAY WASTED ALL ALONE,
I JUMP INTO MY BED AND COVER MY HEAD,
THEN SAY TO MYSELF THIS HAS TO CHANGE
BEFORE I KNOW IT MY HABIT IS GONE,
AND JUST AS I DO THIS,
I KNOW WHAT MUST BE DONE,
I CAN'T LIVE WITH THIS HABIT ANY MORE,
SO THIS HABIT I HAVE MADE MUST
LEAVE AND NEVER COME BACK,
AND I SOON NOTICE HOW QUICKLY I HAVE CHANGED,
AND AM LEARNING TO FIND THE REAL ME AGAIN,
WHICH IS JUST TO HAVE FUN FOR THE HERE AND
NOW AND BE ABLE TO LIVE FOR TODAY HOORAY.

I SAW THE BRIDGE AND WHAT DID I SEE

I SAW THE BRIDGE AND WHAT DID I SEE,
THE END OF THE RAINBOW STARING AT ME,
I START TO WALK WITH FEAR IN MY HEART,
I DO NOT KNOW I WILL FIND WHEN I START,
I START TO COUNT IN MY HEAD,
ONE STEP, TWO, THREE AND FOUR,
THE BRIDGE IS HERE NOW IN THE DUSKY DARK, AS I
THINK TO MYSELF HOW FAR DOES IT GO WHEN I START,
I NOTICE THE CRACK IN THE BRIDGE AS I WALK ALONG,
LIKE THE CRACKS IN MY HEART BATTERED, AND BRUISED,
I MUST BE STRONG AND CONTINUE ON,
I HAVE TO PROVE MY HEART IS TRUE AND STRONG,
EACH STEP I TAKE IS HEAVY ON MY HEART,
BUT ALL I HAVE IN SIGHT IS THE RAINBOW
AT THE END OF THE NIGHT,
THEN I FEEL MY HEART START TO BECOME LIGHTER,
WHEN I FINALLY HAVE MADE IT TO THE OTHER SIDE,
I DID IT AT LAST WHICH DID TAKE ALL MY MIGHT,
I CROSSED THE BRIDGE IN THE STARRY NIGHT,
WHICH DID GIVE ME SO MUCH DELIGHT,

THIS HAS GIVEN ME SO MUCH PEACE IN MY HEART,
AS I JUST STARE UP AT THE BEAUTIFUL RAINBOW,
AND SAY I AM FREE AT LAST WHICH
I PREY WILL ALWAYS LAST

IN THE PSYCHIATRIC WARD

OH NO I GOT SECTIONED AGAIN,
ALL I REALLY WANTED WAS A FRIEND,
THE C.P.N. TAKES ME IN HER CAR,
AFTER THEY GOT A CALL FROM A PASSER BUY,
MY C.P.N. TAKES ME TO HOSPITAL AT NIGHT,
THE SILENCE IS SO STILL WHICH DOES GIVE ME A FRIGHT,
I'M IN HOSPITAL ONCE MORE,
IT IS REALLY DARK IT MUST BE QUITE LATE AT NIGHT,
I HEAR VOICES AS I ENTER A ROOM,
IT MUST BE THE STAFF AS I GET TOLD TO TAKE A SEAT,
WHAT'S WRONG WITH ME THIS TIME I DO NOT KNOW,
ALL I HEAR ARE QUESTIONS BY THE DOCTOR,
THE DOCTOR SAYS WE ARE SECTIONING HER AGAIN,
TO MY C.P.N. AS SHE THEN LEAVES THE ROOM,
THAT IS ME ON MY OWN EXCEPT FOR THE
DOTER WHO SPEAKS ON THE PHONE,
THEN THE PHONE GET'S PUT DOWN AND
HE TELLS ME TO STAY WHERE I AM,
NEXT THE NURSE COMES IN AND LEADS ME TO A ROOM,
WHERE SHE TAKES MY WEIGHT, BLOODS, AND THEN
TAKES ME TO THE ROOM I WILL BE SLEEPING IN,
THEY TAKE ALL MY POSSESSIONS, AND PUT ME TO BED,

THAT IS WHEN MY DIFFERENT TABLETS START
FROM MORNING TO GOING TO BED,
I DO NOT KNOW HOW LONG I AM IN
HOSPITAL IT DOES SEEM BORING,
UNTIL THE DAY THE DOCTOR COMES ROUND
AND TELLS ME I CAN GO HOME,
TWO DAY'S LATER THAT'S ME HOME,
BUT ALL I NEEDED AND WANTED WAS A FRIEND,
SO IF YOU KNOW SOMEONE WITH
MENTAL HEALTH PROBLEMS,
POP IN AND SEE THEM EVEN JUST FOR A CHAT,
SO THEY DON'T FEEL LONELY AND SCARED,
AND ONE DAY THEY CAN LOOK AT YOU AND
SAY WOW I REALLY DO HAVE A FRIEND

PURPOSE

I sit in the night and cry from my heart,
What is the purpose of me being here?
I look at the past and think, what I've done?
All I see is all the years that have gone,
The more I do this the more time I waist,
Then I think what the purpose of all this mess is,
I can't stop thinking,
I'm sure my head will explode,
If I don't stop thinking like this my time will be gone,
So I start to go with the flow,
But what do I see is
Panic, Stress and Frustration,
And so much fear,
So I will stop and listen to the world around,
Then my purpose is to do one thing at a time,
From boiling a kettle, to getting a degree,
It really doesn't matter,
My purpose is to be me,
Then I will have contentment in my heart,
and know my purpose is just to start.

THE FEAR IN MY HEART

—◦◦◦◦◦◦◦◦◦◦—

THE FEAR IN MY HEART IS QUITE UNREAL,
WHAT DO I WHEN THIS FEELING COMES REAL,
I REALLY DON'T KNOW WHAT HE WILL DO,
FROM WHEN I GET UP TILL I GO TO BED,
IM SURE MY HEART IS BEATING TO FAST,
YET WHO WOULD CARE IF I LIVED OR DIED,
THEN HE ENTERS THE ROOM I LOOK AT HIS FACE,
THE ANGER I SEE MAKES ME FREEZE,
I CAN'T BELIEVE THIS IS REAL,
I AM SURE I WILL WAKE AS IT MUST BE A DREAM,
I THEN REALIZE IT IS REAL,
AND I RUN TO THE FRONT DOOR AS QUICK AS I CAN,
BUT HE BEATS ME BEFORE I GET TO THE FONT DOOR,
A FIST IN THE FACE AND A KICK IN THE HEAD,
I HAVE NOW PASSED OUT GOD KNOWS FOR HOW LONG,
I WAKE UP MUCH LATER ON,
HOW LONG HAS PASSED THIS I DON'T KNOW,
BUT WHEN I DID THERE WAS NO ONE THERE,
I THINK TO MYSELF I HAVE TO BE FREE,
SO I RUN TO THE FRONT DOOR BUT THE DOOR IS LOCKED,
NO KEY I POSSESS HE SAY'S THIS IS FOR MY SAFETY
I DON T KNOW HOW LONG IT S BEEN,

TILL I HEAR THE CREEK OF THE FRONT DOOR,
I DARE NOT LOOK UP,
AS MY WHOLE BODY SHAKES,
THEN A SOFT HAND STROKES MY FACE,
A HAND UNDER MY CHIN, MAKES MY EYES GAZE UP,
IN A SOFT AND GENTLE VOICE,
HE SAY'S I HAVE BOUGHT SOME FLOWERS,
AS THEY REMIND ME OF YOU,
THEN BEFORE I KNOW IT THE PAIN HAS GONE,
I HAVE GOT BACK THE KIND MAN WHO LOVES ME AGAIN,
BUT THIS GOES ON FOR SO MANY MONTHS,
I HAVE BY THIS POINT LOST WHO I AM,
UNTIL THE DAY AN AMBULANCE AND
THE POLICE COME TO MY HOUSE,
I END UP IN HOSPITAL ALL I REMEMBER
IS I MUST HAVE PASSED OUT,
I REALIZED I WAS LUCKY THIS TIME
BUT I DID NOT KNOW WHEN
THIS LUCK WOULD END,
I KNEW FOR SURE MY LUCK WOULD END SOON,
AND THIS IS WHEN I REALIZED I HAD
TO GET BACK MY LIFE AGAIN,
I KNEW IN MY HEART I HAD MADE THE START,
OF GETTING MY FREEDOM BACK TO
AND MAKE THAT NEW START,
WHAT AN AMAZING FEELING I GOT THAT NO
ONE COULD TAKE BACK WHAT I HAD LOST,

AND THE ONLY THING I CAN SAY IS
THAT'S ME FREE AT LAST,
WITH ONLY LOVE, JOY AND HAPPINESS
AND NO MORE FEAR,

THE LORD OF THE MANNER

I passed the castle so many times,
Wandered with curiosity every time,
I had to go in this I knew,
As my imagination grew and grew,
I woke up one morning and said in my head,
This is the day I will see for myself,
I arrived at the castle, my heart beating so fast,
When I looked at the door not open till one,
I had fifteen minutes to get inside,
So I went to investigate around the grounds,
What a view from outside,
I just wanted to get inside,
I went back to the door as ten minutes had past,
Then suddenly I felt like I had gone back to the past,
I rang the bell which did give me a thrill,
How grand I felt, when I stood outside the big old door,
I must have been waiting for two or three minutes,
But to me it seemed like forever,
At this time it was like Christmas,
Waiting to open my first present from under the tree,
The grand old door I touched with my hands,
Feeling all the memories come through my hands,
I felt like I was in fairy tale land,

The door slowly opened,
There I was welcomed by two amazing hound dogs,
What a welcome, and how excited I got,
Then my eyes slowly gazed up to see this strong friendly face,
Come in come in was what I heard,
So I followed with so much excitement which felt so surreal,
There I was in the past,
Wow it was like I had gone back in time,
I could feel people round me but not like me they
were so special and from another time,
I felt like a child my brain could not stop I had to
know everything without a second to stop
My heart by this time was flying through
every room and every stone,
So many memories through the castle where to begin,
I felt the happiness, sadness, fear and pain
through the walls, ceilings and floors,
The feeling I felt was like a child so many
questions but so little time,
The Lord of the manner was so kind
And I always enjoy and have questions each time we meet,
He is a man, who will remain in my heart as I
enjoyed listening to him right from the start,
Then it was time to go as I left I said my
goodbyes gave a warm handshake,
I then said to myself I will return to my castle from the past,
To the Lord of the manner who touched my heart,
I believe he is the protector and keeper of this beautiful place,

But to me he is my Merlin to my special fairyland place,
So I will leave you now with a smile in my heat,
And that's where you and my fairytale castle
will remain in my always in my heart.

MY DAD

Where have all the years gone,
This I sadly do not know,
How can time go so fast yet seem so slow,
I'm sure it did go so fast for my Dad,
One minute in a pram, then in the next I
was grown and also left home,
I used to see the confusion of the wonder of time in my Dad's eyes,
Sometimes it did bring a tear to my eyes,
Dad never spoke much to me, but yet I looked
in his eyes and that was enough for me,
I knew my Dad more than he would have ever known,
Which I rely thinks confused him, and defiantly me,
But now he has gone I do wish him peace, and hope
my Dad knew what he rely meant to me,
So now you have left this place called earth,
Please know I was so proud of being able to call you my dad,
I will give you a part of my heart for you to take away,
Till we meet again so I can try and remove all your pain

WHAT HAPPENED TO MUMMY

Mummy, Mummy, where are you
As the police and ambulance enters the house,
I see her lying there on the floor,
But does not move any more,
Five or six police have dragged daddy away,
As I cry in the corner not wanting to move,
I have wet myself and not made it to the loo,
I get held on to this strange but kind lady,
Who hugged me and said hush,
I was so frightened but just held this lady tight
As I hear my daddy shouts so loud,
He always shouts when he drinks too much,
And always hurts mummy and makes her cry,
But this time no more tears,
Just daddy been lifted by five or six police,
Oh the silence in the room makes me scared,
She lifts my mummy from the ground,
But she does not make a sound,
The ambulance man I here say sorry she's gone,
The lady takes me and says come with me
I try and hold mummies hand,
But she is gone and I don't understand,
We go to my grannies to stay there for the night,

She is really nice but not quite right,
So we go to a ladies house, who I do not know,
And got told you will stay here for the night,
In the morning the lady comes back,
I hold her hand and say am I going home
to see mummy in my own home,
The lady looked down and said daddy
is gone and mummy is dead,
But she has now become a star in the sky,
Who always be by your side,
So when you need her just look in the sky,
And your mummy will always be with you and kiss you goodnight,
So please when you read this don't make this real,
Make sure you believe in yourself,
And are dearly you are loved,
Just being you makes you free.
Which will always be enough,

GOODBYE FOR NOW MUM

My Mum might not have always been near but was always hear,
All I had to do was pick up the phone,
My mum was there to try and understand,
Always had a listening ear just sometimes
not the answer I wanted to hear,
But now is the time to say goodbye,
I rely did not know what to say,
As once I said these words goodbye,
I would not be able to pretend she was still alive,
Not pretend she was busy round the house,
Or gone out shopping and just out and about,
So now I say goodbye to my Mum I will rely never forget,
I now hope and pray you have gone to be with dad,
Who will be glad to have you back?
So rest for a little while with peace in your heart,
And know my love for you will never part

THE STARS

The stars in the night do seem so bright,
Which makes me feel like I have a warm blanket
wrapped tight to protect my precious soul?
I do dread when the night come to an end,
As then I have to be strong and attempt to carry on,
When the night eventually ends, and the sun begins to appear,
My mind starts to fret as what will this new day bring,
So when it's time to get up,
I just go straight into the shower which does
seem to give me so much power,
From coping with little things, like the ring on
the phone to the knock on the front door,
I then get dressed and fed,
Oh my how my whole body seems to start to shake,
It is like I am now an old broken down car
that doesn't seem to get very far,
How will I carry on?
Then a wee tiny voice in my head speaks
so softly I can hardly hear,
So I stop and listen come on come on be strong you can carry on,
Then I begin to notice my body slowly stops shaking,
Wow I begin to feel great,
At long last I listen to my voice inside and say I do believe,
I am not weak I am me and that is now good enough for me.

ON THE TRAIN

I cannot wait to get on the train when it comes along,
Oh I am so glad it has not rained,
What if I get there and the train is gone,
I would just have to turn around and go home,
My parents would have had everything prepared,
All these thoughts keep running through my head,
Soon I see the train in the distance,
What a relief as also my panic does leave me,
I did shout out with big sigh of relief,
Wow how glad I am to still be alive,
I step on the busy train with my bag as well,
Then quickly walk down the narrow aisle,
My number of seat I have found at last,
Then sit in the very bumpy train seat,
There are many children around making such a noise,
So I put on my headphones and have a little sleep,
When I reach London Town I get to know all the
friends and family I have been longing to see,
What fun we have for two or three days,
With an extra suitcase containing all the memories we have made,
To take back to my home which is in Fife?

THE FOUR SEASONS OF LIFE

The birds start nesting in the hedges and also the trees,
The leaves start budding before the flowers come out,
New life starts to enter our beautiful earth,
A start of a new beginning for everyone,
Even the old start to have fun,
People start to smile at each other where ever we go,
A little bit nervous but just want to explore,
Thinking what is behind that brand new door,
Then summer shows herself to the world,
We all by now have a good idea where we have chosen to go,
And life starts to feel rely great,
Without a care in the world we put our
first foot on our path called life,
Some are straight so you can see all the way to the end,
Some with so many twist and turns a bit like a roller coaster,
But we all choose for our self which one to go,
Chicks and the lamb have all started to grow,
The country side is now lush and green,
Babies have all started too grown,
We all at this point think we know it all,
But do not notice the clock ticking our time away,
Before we know it autumn has shown her face,
The colours on the tree turn to beautiful copper shades,

Now everything is where it should be,
But we do not notice things are just beginning to slow down,
All we see is that we all have found and in our roll in life,
We do see the clock tick from the corner of our eye,
We all choose to ignore this and say we have plenty of time,
As in our heads it is still spring and all want to play,
We don't notice winter shows her face,
Wow the cold has gone through all of our bones,
The trees are covered with a white blanket of snow,
The grass has stopped for a little rest,
The geese have flown to a warmer place,
But will return when the sun returns,
People by this point are at old age as they see the clock tick away,
They by this point wonder where time has gone,
You see panic as they lay down in their bed,
Then notice a mirror next to them
So they pick it up and look at the face
and with a big gasp of shock,
Realize this whole story was all about them
just as they take their last breath,
The mirror slowly falls gently to the ground,
As in the next room a new life has arrived
to start the new cycle of life,
The baby looks out the window and sees all the geese appearing,

ANGELS IN MY HEART

I walked along the winding road one day,
That they would here my heart cry out,
So they could listen to the truth from within,
As all I longed for at this point,
Was for the pain to be removed from my heart,
Where my heart could now be filled with love,
As I then walked around the corner of
this long and winding road,
Stood the angel who had all the answers to my prayers,
I knew at this moment my heart would soon be cured,
So I took a deep breath and approached
my Angel who was waiting there,
And suddenly I felt a glow healing all the pain from my heart,
What an amazing feeling I got from inside to out,
This was the start for me to have faith, Hope,
Love and start to live without the pain.

BOXES

I hate living, but I don't want to die,
I wish I could be normal,
But what is normal I say,
Then from deep inside all I want is to be
loved and give the same back,
Then I say in my mind why does it rely have to be
with a man, Why can it not be for love?
As we are all human and all need Love well that's
what they say makes the world go round,
Why does it have to be with women?
Why can it not be just for love?
As we are all human and all need love well that's what they say.
Why is there so many boxes people put
everyone in even themselves
Sayings are you straight,
Are you gay and of course all the rest,
Why can't you be allowed to love the person for just being them?
Why can't you love yourself for just being you?
But in this world most people feel safe with
putting each other in boxes,
That even includes them self's
So when people come up and say who are you?
I Just say I am me please to meat you. Have a nice day.

THE DAY I MET YOU

THE day I met you my heart became alive,
It was like I reached out and an angel touched my heart,
How my soul suddenly was free at last,
It was you the Angel, who took away the pain,
It was you, who made my heart free and young again,
After all these years that have passed,
I have always had a part of you keeping my dreams alive,
Even when I had lost all my hope to stay alive,
You had kept part of me safe where no one could see,
Not even you or me,
So when we met up many years later on,
My love for you had grown and grown,
So if we are ever apart you will always have
that special place in my heart,
Which keeps my soul alive?

THE DAY I UNDERSTAND
I AM ME

I look at everyone in the past,
Then say to myself how nasty they are,
Always seem to be talking about one another,
Yet they all seem to get along,
I did used to wander why people thought I was rely dumb,
Then I did notice it was not them who thought this way
It was me looking in that mirror in my head just talking to me,
Oh how I did berate myself all the time,
So in the end I had no name,
Now no longer did I say why they do not listen,
I said why I don't listen,
So if you ever go on about the person you do not like,
Look in your mirror as it might be you,
If this is the case stop for a moment give yourself a hug,
And just say to your heart I am rely full of love,
Who is now able to give and receive all I rely want and need,
Now I rely do feel at long last me